# MAKING A CAR

GW00771677

by Claire Llewellyn

illustrated by Jonatronix

CAMBRIDGE
UNIVERSITY PRESS

UCL
Institute of Education

# The car factory

The machines that help us to build the cars are called **robots**.

This is a car **factory**.

Lots of cars are made here.

Lots of people work here.

Cars are made by **workers** and machines.

③

## Step 1: Cutting the steel

Cars are made out of **steel**.

Big rolls of steel are made into flat sheets.

Then machines bend the sheets and cut them into the parts of a car.

## Step 2: Making the body

This is called **welding**.

Robots heat up the steel parts.

The steel gets so hot that it begins to **melt**.

Then the parts can be joined together to make the body of the car.

# Step 3: Painting the body

The car is painted to stop it **rusting**.

First it is dipped into a pool of grey paint.

The last coat of paint is shiny so that the car looks great!

When the car is dry, the robots spray on three more coats of paint.

Each coat needs to dry before the next one goes on.

## Step 4: Fitting the engine

The next part to fit is the **engine**.

It is the most important part of the car.

Engines are very heavy so the robots lift them in.

## Step 5: Fitting the parts

Next, the car moves along a moving belt.

It is called the **assembly line**.

The belt stops now and then so that the workers can fit a new part into the car.

Each car is different. A list tells the workers which parts to fit.

13

# Step 6: Checking the car

Now every part of the car is checked.

Every part must look good and work well.

Then the car is ready to leave the factory.

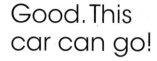

Good. This car can go!

**CHECKLIST**

The body ✓
The paint ✓
The engine ✓
The brakes ✓
The lights ✓
The horn ✓
The wipers ✓
The windows

# Glossary

**assembly line**   line of workers and machines in a factory

**engine**   part of a car that makes it move

**factory**   place where goods are made

**melt**   become soft or runny when heated

**robots**   machines that moves and can do some jobs

**rusting**   when metal turns brown and starts to break

**steel**   very strong type of metal

**welding**   when two bits of metal are joined by heating them until they melt

**workers**   people who work

# Making a Car ✦ Claire Llewellyn

Reading notes written by Sue Bodman and Glen Franklin

## Using this book

### Developing reading comprehension

This non-fiction text takes us through the process of making a car. Technical terms are well-defined and the layout offers lots of opportunities to learn how to use simple non-fiction features such as a glossary and captions.

### Grammar and sentence structure

- Use of chronological presentation and vocabulary, such as 'First', 'Next', 'Then' and 'Now'.
- Impersonal sentence structures in keeping with non-fiction genre.

### Word meaning and spelling

- Two and three syllable words to develop decoding skills (for example, 'factory', 'assembly', 'machines', 'robots').

### Curriculum links

*Design Technology* – Design cars; children could use junk modelling and construction toys to build their cars after designing.

*Science* – Children could explore materials (wood, metal, paper, plastic, etc.) for their various properties and qualities.

## Learning Outcomes

### Children can:

- solve new words using print information and understanding of the text
- understand how a procedural text works.

## A guided reading lesson

### Book Introduction

Give each child a copy of the book and read the title.

### Orientation

Give a brief overview of the book, using language appropriate for procedural texts: *This book takes us through the process of making a car. It tells us about where a car is made and the steps that need to be followed.* Make links with any other procedural texts that the children have read previously.

### Preparation

Page 2: Make sure the children understand that the headings must be read in a non-fiction text. Revise the use of the bold words. Draw their attention to the commentary provided by the mechanic character. Focus on the word *'robots'* in the caption. Ask the children to explain what a robot is – make sure they know that the machines in the factory are called robots.

Page 4: Read the heading aloud and ask the children to read it too. Note the word *'steel'* is emboldened. Support the children to decode the word, saying it slowly. Explain that this indicates the word meaning is included in the glossary. Say: *Let's find out what 'steel' is.* Turn to the back page and read aloud the definition. Then tell the children that if they do not understand the meaning of one of the bold words, they can go to the glossary to find out. Ask: *Can you see the robots in this picture? What are they doing?* Reinforce the vocabulary *'flat sheets'*, *'bend'* and *'cut'*.

Page 6: Read the heading aloud. Ask: *Can you see the robots in this picture? What are they doing now?*

Ask the children what else they think needs to be done to make a car. Take some responses, maybe asking children to discuss in pairs before sharing in the group.

Set a purpose for reading: *This book shows us how a car is made. There are six steps. When you have finished reading, we will see if we can remember the order of the jobs the robots need to do.*